Wedding Planner
Mr ♥ Mrs

Wedding Planner...

♡

WEDDING DATE & TIME:

VENUE ADDRESS:

BUDGET:

OFFICIANT:

WEDDING PARTY:

NOTES & REMINDERS:

TO DO LIST:

Wedding Budget...

	TOTAL COST:	DEPOSIT:	REMAINDER:
WEDDING VENUE			
RECEPTION VENUE			
FLORIST			
OFFICIANT			
CATERER			
WEDDING CAKE			
BRIDAL ATTIRE			
GROOM ATTIRE			
BRIDAL JEWELRY			
BRIDESMAID ATTIRE			
GROOMSMEN ATTIRE			
HAIR & MAKE UP			
PHOTOGRAPHER			
VIDEOGRAPHER			
DJ SERVICE/ENTERTAINMENT			
INVITATIONS			
TRANSPORTATION			
WEDDING PARTY GIFTS			
RENTALS			
HONEYMOON			

12 Months Before...

SET THE DATE

SET YOUR BUDGET

CHOOSE YOUR THEME

ORGANIZE ENGAGEMENT PARTY

RESEARCH VENUES

BOOK A WEDDING PLANNER

RESEARCH PHOTOGRAPHERS

RESEARCH VIDEOGRAPHERS

RESEARCH DJ'S/ENTERTAINMENT

CONSIDER FLORISTS

RESEARCH CATERERS

DECIDE ON OFFICIANT

CREATE INITIAL GUEST LIST

CHOOSE WEDDING PARTY

SHOP FOR WEDDING DRESS

REGISTER WITH GIFT REGISTRY

DISCUSS HONEYMOON IDEAS

RESEARCH WEDDING RINGS

THINGS TO REMEMBER:

DATE:

9 Months Before...

- FINALIZE GUEST LIST
- ORDER INVITATIONS
- PLAN YOUR RECEPTION
- BOOK PHOTOGRAPHER
- BOOK VIDEOGRAPHER
- BOOK FLORIST
- BOOK DJ/ENTERTAINMENT
- BOOK CATERER
- CHOOSE WEDDING CAKE

- CHOOSE WEDDING GOWN
- ORDER BRIDESMAIDS DRESSES
- RESERVE TUXEDOS
- ARRANGE TRANSPORTATION
- BOOK WEDDING VENUE
- BOOK RECEPTION VENUE
- PLAN HONEYMOON
- BOOK OFFICIANT
- BOOK ROOMS FOR GUESTS

THINGS TO REMEMBER:

DATE:

6 Months Before...

- ORDER THANK YOU NOTES
- REVIEW RECEPTION DETAILS
- MAKE APPT FOR DRESS FITTING
- CONFIRM BRIDEMAIDS DRESSES
- GET MARRIAGE LICENSE

- BOOK HAIR/MAKE UP STYLIST
- CONFIRM MUSIC SELECTIONS
- PLAN BRIDAL SHOWER
- PLAN REHEARSAL
- SHOP FOR WEDDING RINGS

THINGS TO REMEMBER:

DATE:

3 Months Before...

- MAIL OUT INVITATIONS
- MEET WITH OFFICIANT
- BUY GIFTS FOR WEDDING PARTY
- BOOK FINAL GOWN FITTING
- BUY WEDDING BANDS
- PLAN YOUR HAIR STYLE
- PURCHASE SHOES/HEELS
- CONFIRM PASSPORTS ARE VALID

- FINALIZE RECEPTION MENU
- PLAN REHEARSAL DINNER
- CONFIRM ALL BOOKINGS
- APPLY FOR MARRIAGE LICENSE
- CONFIRM MUSIC SELECTIONS
- DRAFT WEDDING VOWS
- CHOOSE YOUR MC
- ARRANGE AIRPORT TRANSFER

THINGS TO REMEMBER:

1 Month Before...

- CONFIRM FINAL GUEST COUNT
- CONFIRM RECEPTION DETAILS
- ATTEND FINAL GOWN FITTING
- CONFIRM PHOTOGRAPHER
- WRAP WEDDING PARTY GIFTS
- CREATE PHOTOGRAPHY SHOT LIST

- REHEARSE WEDDING VOWS
- BOOK MANI-PEDI
- CONFIRM WITH FLORIST
- CONFIRM VIDEOGRAPHER
- PICK UP BRIDEMAIDS DRESSES
- CREATE WEDDING SCHEDULE

THINGS TO REMEMBER:

DATE:

1 Week Before...

- FINALIZE SEATING PLANS
- MAKE PAYMENTS TO VENDORS
- PACK FOR HONEYMOON
- CONFIRM HOTEL RESERVATIONS
- GIVE SCHEDULE TO PARTY

- DELIVER LICENSE TO OFFICIANT
- CONFIRM WITH BAKERY
- PICK UP WEDDING DRESS
- PICK UP TUXEDOS
- GIVE MUSIC LIST TO DJ

THINGS TO REMEMBER:

DATE:

The Day Before...

- [ ] GET MANICURE/PEDICURE
- [ ] ATTEND REHEARSAL DINNER
- [ ] GET A GOOD NIGHT'S SLEEP!

- [ ] GIVE GIFTS TO WEDDING PARTY
- [ ] FINALIZE PACKING

TO DO LIST:

DATE:

Wedding Planner...

ENGAGEMENT PARTY:

DATE: _____

TIME: _____

LOCATION: _____

NUMBER OF GUESTS: _____

NOTES:

BRIDAL SHOWER:

DATE: _____

TIME: _____

LOCATION: _____

NUMBER OF GUESTS: _____

NOTES:

STAG & DOE PARTY:

DATE: _____

TIME: _____

LOCATION: _____

NUMBER OF GUESTS: _____

NOTES:

Wedding Party

MAID/MATRON OF HONOR:

PHONE: _____ DRESS SIZE: _____ SHOE SIZE: _____

EMAIL: _____

BRIDESMAID:

PHONE: _____ DRESS SIZE: _____ SHOE SIZE: _____

EMAIL: _____

BRIDESMAID #2:

PHONE: _____ DRESS SIZE: _____ SHOE SIZE: _____

EMAIL: _____

BRIDESMAID #3:

PHONE: _____ DRESS SIZE: _____ SHOE SIZE: _____

EMAIL: _____

BRIDESMAID #4:

PHONE: _____ DRESS SIZE: _____ SHOE SIZE: _____

EMAIL: _____

Wedding Party

BEST MAN:

PHONE: _____ WAIST SIZE: _____ SHOE SIZE: _____

NECK SIZE: _____ SLEEVE SIZE: _____ JACKET SIZE: _____

EMAIL: _____

GROOMSMEN #1:

PHONE: _____ WAIST SIZE: _____ SHOE SIZE: _____

NECK SIZE: _____ SLEEVE SIZE: _____ JACKET SIZE: _____

EMAIL: _____

GROOMSMEN #2:

PHONE: _____ WAIST SIZE: _____ SHOE SIZE: _____

NECK SIZE: _____ SLEEVE SIZE: _____ JACKET SIZE: _____

EMAIL: _____

GROOMSMEN #3:

PHONE: _____ WAIST SIZE: _____ SHOE SIZE: _____

NECK SIZE: _____ SLEEVE SIZE: _____ JACKET SIZE: _____

EMAIL: _____

GROOMSMEN #4:

PHONE: _____ WAIST SIZE: _____ SHOE SIZE: _____

NECK SIZE: _____ SLEEVE SIZE: _____ JACKET SIZE: _____

EMAIL: _____

Photographer

PHOTOGRAPHER:

PHONE: _____   COMPANY: _____

EMAIL: _____   ADDRESS: _____

_____

WEDDING PACKAGE OVERVIEW:

EST PRICE: _____

INCLUSIONS: YES ✓   NO ✓   COST:

ENGAGEMENT SHOOT: _____

PHOTO ALBUMS: _____

FRAMES: _____

PROOFS INCLUDED: _____

NEGATIVES INCLUDED: _____

TOTAL COST: _____

Videographer

VIDEOGRAPHER:

PHONE: _____   COMPANY: _____

EMAIL: _____   ADDRESS: _____

_____

_____

WEDDING PACKAGE OVERVIEW:

EST PRICE: _____

INCLUSIONS:	YES ✓	NO ✓	COST:
DUPLICATES/COPIES:	☐	☐	_____
PHOTO MONTAGE:	☐	☐	_____
MUSIC ADDED:	☐	☐	_____
EDITING:	☐	☐	_____

TOTAL COST: _____

DJ/Entertainment

DJ/LIVE BAND/ENTERTAINMENT:

PHONE: _____   COMPANY: _____

EMAIL: _____   ADDRESS: _____

START TIME: _____   END TIME: _____

ENTERTAINMENT SERVICE OVERVIEW:

EST PRICE: _____

INCLUSIONS: YES ✓   NO ✓   COST:

SOUND EQUIPMENT: _____

LIGHTING: _____

SPECIAL EFFECTS: _____

GRATUITIES

TOTAL COST: _____

Florist Planner

FLORIST:

PHONE: _____   COMPANY: _____

EMAIL: _____   ADDRESS: _____

FLORAL PACKAGE:

EST PRICE: _____

INCLUSIONS:	YES ✓	NO ✓	COST:
BRIDAL BOUQUET:			_____
THROW AWAY BOUQUET:			_____
CORSAGES:			_____
CEREMONY FLOWERS			_____
CENTERPIECES			_____
CAKE TOPPER			_____
BOUTONNIERE			_____

TOTAL COST:

Wedding Cake

PHONE: _____   COMPANY: _____

EMAIL: _____   ADDRESS: _____

WEDDING CAKE PACKAGE:

♡

COST: _____   FREE TASTING: _____   DELIVERY FEE: _____

FLAVOR: _____

FILLING: _____

SIZE: _____

SHAPE: _____

COLOR: _____

EXTRAS: _____

TOTAL COST: _____

Transportation Planner

TO CEREMONY: PICK UP TIME: PICK UP LOCATION:

BRIDE: _____

GROOM: _____

BRIDE'S PARENTS: _____

GROOM'S PARENTS: _____

BRIDESMAIDS: _____

GROOMSMEN: _____

NOTES:

TO RECEPTION: PICK UP TIME: PICK UP LOCATION:

BRIDE & GROOM: _____

BRIDE'S PARENTS: _____

GROOM'S PARENTS: _____

BRIDESMAIDS: _____

GROOMSMEN: _____

Wedding Planner...

BACHELORETTE PARTY:

DATE: _____   LOCATION: _____

TIME: _____   NUMBER OF GUESTS: _____

NOTES:

BACHELOR PARTY:

DATE: _____   LOCATION: _____

TIME: _____   NUMBER OF GUESTS: _____

NOTES:

CEREMONY REHEARSAL:

DATE: _____   LOCATION: _____

TIME: _____   NUMBER OF GUESTS: _____

NOTES:

Wedding Planner...

REHEARSAL DINNER:

DATE: _____   LOCATION: _____

TIME: _____   NUMBER OF GUESTS: _____

NOTES:

RECEPTION:

DATE: _____   LOCATION: _____

TIME: _____   NUMBER OF GUESTS: _____

NOTES:

REMINDERS:

_____

_____

_____

_____

_____

Names & Addresses

CEREMONY:

PHONE: _____   CONTACT NAME: _____

EMAIL: _____   ADDRESS: _____

RECEPTION:

PHONE: _____   CONTACT NAME: _____

EMAIL: _____   ADDRESS: _____

OFFICIANT:

PHONE: _____   CONTACT NAME: _____

EMAIL: _____   ADDRESS: _____

WEDDING PLANNER:

PHONE: _____   CONTACT NAME: _____

EMAIL: _____   ADDRESS: _____

Names & Addresses

CATERER:

PHONE: _____   CONTACT NAME: _____

EMAIL: _____   ADDRESS: _____

FLORIST:

PHONE: _____   CONTACT NAME: _____

EMAIL: _____   ADDRESS: _____

BAKERY:

PHONE: _____   CONTACT NAME: _____

EMAIL: _____   ADDRESS: _____

BRIDAL SHOP:

PHONE: _____   CONTACT NAME: _____

EMAIL: _____   ADDRESS: _____

Names & Addresses

PHOTOGRAPHER:

PHONE: _____   CONTACT NAME: _____

EMAIL: _____   ADDRESS: _____

VIDEOGRAPHER:

PHONE: _____   CONTACT NAME: _____

EMAIL: _____   ADDRESS: _____

DJ/ENTERTAINMENT:

PHONE: _____   CONTACT NAME: _____

EMAIL: _____   ADDRESS: _____

HAIR/NAIL SALON:

PHONE: _____   CONTACT NAME: _____

EMAIL: _____   ADDRESS: _____

Names & Addresses

MAKE UP ARTIST:

PHONE: _____   CONTACT NAME: _____

EMAIL: _____   ADDRESS: _____

RENTALS:

PHONE: _____   CONTACT NAME: _____

EMAIL: _____   ADDRESS: _____

HONEYMOON RESORT/HOTEL:

PHONE: _____   CONTACT NAME: _____

EMAIL: _____   ADDRESS: _____

TRANSPORTATION SERVICE:

PHONE: _____   CONTACT NAME: _____

EMAIL: _____   ADDRESS: _____

Caterer Details

CONTACT INFORMATION:

PHONE: _____   CONTACT NAME: _____

EMAIL: _____   ADDRESS: _____

MENU CHOICE #1:

MENU CHOICE #2:

	YES ✓	NO ✓	COST:
BAR INCLUDED:			_____
CORKAGE FEE:			_____
HORS D'OEURS:			_____
TAXES INCLUDED:			_____
GRATUITIES INCLUDED:			_____

Menu Planner

HORS D'OEUVRES

1st COURSE:

2nd COURSE:

3rd COURSE:

4th COURSE:

DESSERT:

Menu Planner

COFFEE/TEA:

FRUIT:

SWEETS TABLE:

WEDDING CAKE:

NOTES:

1 Week Before...

	THINGS TO DO:	NOTES:
MONDAY		
TUESDAY		
WEDNESDAY		
THURSDAY		

REMINDERS & NOTES:

1 Week Before...

	THINGS TO DO:	NOTES:
FRIDAY		
SATURDAY		
SUNDAY		

LEFT TO DO:

REMINDERS:

NOTES:

DATE:

DATE:

Wedding Guest List

NAME:	ADDRESS:	# IN PARTY:	RSVP: ✓

Wedding Guest List

NAME:	ADDRESS:	# IN PARTY:	RSVP: ✓

Wedding Guest List

NAME:	ADDRESS:	# IN PARTY:	RSVP: ✓

Wedding Guest List

NAME:	ADDRESS:	# IN PARTY:	RSVP: ✓

Wedding Guest List

NAME:	ADDRESS:	# IN PARTY:	RSVP: ✓

Wedding Guest List

NAME:	ADDRESS:	# IN PARTY:	RSVP: ✓

Wedding Guest List

NAME:	ADDRESS:	# IN PARTY:	RSVP: ✓

Wedding Guest List

NAME:	ADDRESS:	# IN PARTY:	RSVP: ✓

Wedding Guest List

NAME:	ADDRESS:	# IN PARTY:	RSVP: ✓

Wedding Guest List

NAME:	ADDRESS:	# IN PARTY:	RSVP: ✓

Wedding Guest List

NAME:	ADDRESS:	# IN PARTY:	RSVP: ✓

Wedding Guest List

NAME:	ADDRESS:	# IN PARTY:	RSVP: ✓

Wedding Guest List

NAME:	ADDRESS:	# IN PARTY:	RSVP: ✓

Wedding Guest List

NAME:	ADDRESS:	# IN PARTY:	RSVP: ✓

Wedding Guest List

NAME:	ADDRESS:	# IN PARTY:	RSVP: ✓

Wedding Guest List

NAME:	ADDRESS:	# IN PARTY:	RSVP: ✓

Wedding Guest List

NAME:	ADDRESS:	# IN PARTY:	RSVP: ✓

Wedding Guest List

NAME:	ADDRESS:	# IN PARTY:	RSVP: ✓

Wedding Guest List

NAME:	ADDRESS:	# IN PARTY:	RSVP: ✓

Wedding Guest List

NAME:	ADDRESS:	# IN PARTY:	RSVP: ✓

Wedding Guest List

NAME:	ADDRESS:	# IN PARTY:	RSVP: ✓

Wedding Guest List

NAME:	ADDRESS:	# IN PARTY:	RSVP: ✓

Wedding Guest List

NAME:	ADDRESS:	# IN PARTY:	RSVP: ✓

Wedding Guest List

NAME:	ADDRESS:	# IN PARTY:	RSVP: ✓

Wedding Guest List

NAME:	ADDRESS:	# IN PARTY:	RSVP: ✓

Wedding Guest List

NAME:	ADDRESS:	# IN PARTY:	RSVP: ✓

Wedding Guest List

NAME:	ADDRESS:	# IN PARTY:	RSVP: ✓

Wedding Guest List

NAME:	ADDRESS:	# IN PARTY:	RSVP: ✓

Wedding Guest List

NAME:	ADDRESS:	# IN PARTY:	RSVP: ✓

Wedding Guest List

NAME:	ADDRESS:	# IN PARTY:	RSVP: ✓

Wedding Guest List

NAME:	ADDRESS:	# IN PARTY:	RSVP: ✓

Seating Planner

Table #

Table #

Seating Planner

Table #

Table #

Seating Planner

Table #

Table #

Seating Planner

Table #

Table #

Seating Planner

Table #

Table #

Seating Planner

Table #

Table #

Seating Planner

Table #

Table #

Seating Planner

Table #

Table #

Seating Planner

Table #

Table #

Seating Planner

Table #

Table #

Seating Planner

Table #

Table #

Seating Planner

Table #

Table #

Seating Planner

Table #

Table #

Seating Planner

Table #

Table #

Seating Planner

Table #

Table #

Seating Planner

Table #

Table #

Seating Planner

Table #

Table #

Seating Planner

Table #

Table #

Seating Planner

Table #

Table #

Seating Planner

Table #

Table #

Seating Planner

Table #

Table #

Seating Planner

Table #

Table #

Seating Planner

Table #

Table #

Seating Planner

Table #

Table #

Seating Planner

Table #

Table #

Seating Planner

Table #

Table #

Seating Planner

Table #

Table #

Seating Planner

Table #

Table #

Seating Planner

Table #

Table #

Seating Planner

Table #

Table #

Seating Planner

Table #

Table #

Seating Planner

Table #

Table #

Seating Planner

Table #

Table #

Seating Planner

Table #

Table #

Seating Planner

Table #

Table #

Seating Planner

Table #

Table #

Seating Planner

Table #

Table #

Seating Planner

Table #

Table #

Seating Planner

Table #

Table #

Seating Planner

Table #

Table #

Seating Planner

Table #

Table #

Seating Planner

Table #

Table #

Seating Planner

Table #

Table #

Seating Planner

Table #

Table #

Seating Planner

Table #

Table #

Seating Planner

Table #

Table #

Seating Planner

Table #

Table #

Seating Planner

Table #

Table #

Seating Planner

Table #

Table #

Seating Planner

Table #

Table #

Seating Planner

Table #

Table #

Seating Planner

Table #

Table #

Seating Planner

Table #

Table #

Seating Planner

Table #

Table #

Seating Planner

Table #

Table #

Seating Planner

Table #

Table #

Seating Planner

Table #

Table #

Seating Planner

Table #

Table #

The Big Day!

- [ ] GET HAIR & MAKE UP DONE
- [ ] HAVE A HEALTHY BREAKFAST
- [ ] ENJOY YOUR BIG DAY!
- [ ] MEET WITH BRIDESMAIDS
- [ ] GIVE RINGS TO BEST MAN

TO DO LIST:

Made in the USA
Middletown, DE
04 August 2019